Jubilant Echoes of Silent Love

By Earline Buchanan Pitts

ISBN: 0615430104
ISBN-13: 9780615430102

The Person Within Our Innermost Thoughts Is
But The Reflection Of The Life We Embrace

To: Jeff,
Read for the Journey
Walk it With Love
Commune With Peace !
Enjoy the Reading
Earline Pitts 5-12-2011

Dwell in My Garden
You'll Understand His MERCY & GRACE

As a young girl growing up in Manchester, Georgia, I remember working in the garden pulling weeds, watering tomato plants, digging potatoes, cropping collards, pulling and shucking corn, picking and shelling peas and beans, then spending hours preserving them.

I have always loved flowers and enjoyed popping morning glories and pushing my nose to the center of a sunflower just to get a whiff of the sweet summer aroma.

I never thought that I would be caught working in a garden once I left home and went off to Fort Valley State University. However as fate would have it, I have several small areas of flowers which I call my garden around our home of thirty-five years, where I reside with my husband, Wayne, of forty-two years, and our daughter, Sherlonda.

Amazingly, after the death of our son, Antwain, the flowers became a source of therapy and joy. Once I retired from a fortune 500 company as a Sales Representative and five years after the death of our son, I started slowly getting into maintaining a flower garden.

Working with the flowers has given me a deeper appreciation for the gift of life and all of the elements that affect how we live and interact with those around us. In the country, we just call them flowerbeds, but my small gardens are the inspiration for the gift of writing-- for which I am very thankful to God.

I invite you to "Dwell in My Garden." Walk through the flowerbeds of love, joy, pain and sorrow, then find the flowerbed of happiness and peace, "You'll Understand His Mercy and Grace" and what God's gift of life means to me, interpreted through the writings of this book of poetic expression.

Earline Buchanan Pitts

Forward:

Let our joy rise and forever reign!

This masterpiece of tender and inspirational verse is a must read. Earline Buchanan Pitts has penned a very touching work that will be treasured for a life-time by those who are blessed to experience these emotionally uplifting verses. Earline carefully shares her life lessons on almost every subject of the human experience. She truly is a gifted writer who possesses the artful talent of story-telling in poetry.

Earline's verses help us connect with our inner-self and with those most precious to us.

So, take this journey and discover new peace, tranquility and joy in knowing yourself more deeply and fully. You will enjoy reading and rereading these life treasures. You will come to know more vividly your purpose in life.

Earline's book was three years in the writing. It has been a long journey; but one in which Earline has created a new world for herself and for those around her.

I invite you to experience and absorb the fragrance of this gifted poet. Listen to how you can be drawn ever so closer to those who mean the most to you. They are your most valued treasures.

Earline, thank you for illuminating this path and giving us a must read!

Coach & Editor
Walter Nelms

Dedicated to:

To my dear family and special friends. Each of you means so much to me in the very special way that you already know.

Acknowledgments:

I would like to thank my family and my many friends who assisted and encouraged me to complete this Book of Poetry.

I give the glory to God for He is the fiber of my existence.

Special recognition to my husband, Wayne, who has been such a big support and smiling listener; to my daughter Sherlonda Pitts, whom I love so dearly as she tries to keep me from being too protective of her. To the memory of our beloved son, Antwain, as he departed this life far too early on February 1, 2001-- untouchable but not forgotten.

My Mother, Emily R. Buchanan who is a very strong and determined lady, as are most of the women in the family. To the memory of my father, Claudie Buchanan who passed along his sense of what he referred to as "Mother Wit". To my sisters and brothers, and especially to the memory of my deceased sister, whom I held so often as a child on our front porch, as I watched the other children play. Caring for my siblings taught me responsibility which I learned to accept without resistance. And to all my relatives, in-laws, and friends for the love and smiles shown along the way.

To the many teachers, professors and instructors with whom I crossed paths and particularly Mrs. Ann Banning Warrior, for her influence on my life as I was able to grasp her feeling for the love of literature in high school. Also a special thanks to William "Bill" & Phyllis Cook for being my cheerleaders.

My warmest thanks to Patrice Coleman, Carl Johnson and Frances Pruitt for your wonderful and invaluable assistance in helping with my book cover photo.

To my sisters and brothers in Christ (whom I love so deeply) at the Greenforest Community Baptist Church where we worship.

To Walter and Jackie Nelms from my family to your family-- thanks for being such good friends. Walter, thanks for being such a wonderful colleague and encouraging me to write even when I so adamantly said no--- and thanks for thinking of me as a poet.

I thank God for allowing me to make this journey, and for special circumstances; yes, I am at a point in my life where God can use me, enjoying life as a wife, mother, homemaker, flower gardener, business woman, and poet.

This book of poetry represents my journey, surviving the trials of life to enjoy living life to its fullest and being fulfilled in His Grace.

I give Thanks to God for You all.

Earline Buchanan Pitts

Prelude:

Moments of Fame

The more I write
The deeper secluded
Is the silence of my thoughts
And the muteness of my speech

Thank God
For family and friends as you
Always encouraging me
To color words on paper with pen

So that one day
I may be known
For the eloquence to write
With the tenderness of a smile
God has placed within me

Chapters

Chapter I - Hope In Tomorrow

I.   *Nature's Fall Expression*

Handsome is the grand oak tree
With its vivacious golden orange leaves,
Posing in my neighbor's yard
Glowing and smiling just for me
As though we share awareness
To the goodness of God
In nature, we see.

Intriguing is this time of the year.
Autumn
Shinning under the brilliance of the fall sun
Our spirits are lifted
By the wonderful harvest of aging leaves
The gathering of their bright earthen colors
Nature's expression, to the richness of life

Valuable are the tangibles we touch.
Invaluable is the affectionate love felt
From intangibles secretly held within
Sacred places that we privately portend.

For our heart's conveyance
Of peace and good will
Rejoices in knowing
That The God we serve
Is unmistakably real
And Praised for all creation
Revered for His Sovereignty,
Being a jealous God
Unyieldingly desirous of our love
And sharing His harvest in the end.

2.   ## Winters Come And They Pass

Like a newly sharpened razor
A seasoned butcher's knife
Keenly stationed against
The deep darkness of night
Indiscriminately the piercing silence from beyond
Gave license to enraged tears of fear

Wind blown echoes of urgency became
The ghostly moans of mom-m...
Whistling to my daylight tenebrosity
Soothing the hurt thundering in my uneasy heart.

Unexpected was his tragic demise
One Friday morning before dawn
Forever lost was that soft utterance
Of a loving goodbye
And the kiss of an eternal love

Grief stricken by a crushing wintry blizzard
Listless as a lonesome dove struggling to survive,
Blindly I swirled into a maze of shame
To ease my unsettling spirit
And in the sanctity of seclusion, hide
From doleful reminders of absolute coldness
Confirmation that my loved one died

Seven springs, summers, and falls passed;
Winter's strong hold sustained its frigid blast.
Under His mercy and unfailing love
God patiently kept watch over my shaken soul
While others about me fervently prayed.
And time faithfully motioned me onward
Seconding the minutes of those blackened days.

"Weeping may endure for a night,
But joy cometh in the morning."
(Psalms 30:5, KJV)

The spirit approaches me during my weeping hours
As a glorious shinning light
Magnifying my eyes to the blessings of life
To see, feel and smell
The delightful treasures of joyfulness
Gifts of warmth for my grateful heart

Glitter of diamonds for the birthing of Spring
Sparkle of rubies for the blissful Summer
Twinkle of gold for the mellowness of Fall
Thick and shinny was the bronze chest
Symbolic of the slumberous Winter
Safekeeping its riches for the natural balance
Under which all creatures lodge

Promises of winter the hour will keep
But in our lives thrives
An unanticipated maitre d'
Seating bravely all four
Spring, Summer, Winter and Fall
Seldom ever able to decipher their calls
Joyfully we harmonize with the assurance
Of every peaceful awakening
Paying reverence to God for each;
Certain of His comfort that He Is and Cares.

3. ## Winter Stings For A Moment

A winter's sting likens to a thin paper cut
The deeper the wound
The longer the hurt
Requiring tending and mending
Teary water for cleansing,
Glorious joy for healing

A heart torn has been refashioned
The journey has not ended
God has altered the course
And I have transitioned
To the hope and faith of the righteous
Finding contentment with each season of change

God is my refuge
He is, my Rock and my Fortress
My Liberator for the present and future
My Deliverer from the pains of the past

Winters are only for a moment
They come and they pass
Eternal peace is in Christ
His promise that will forever last

4. ## Loss

Each death bears,
A significant loss
A past sealed in memories,
Lingering in the heart of cherished thoughts

A present life dimmed by darkness
As breath is vaporized to an abrupt halt
A future that within seconds ends
Void of a past and present
Unable to reward tomorrow
With a Good Morning to honor friends.

Formed from earth a transition begins.
Obediently, life awaits and transcends
To rest in peace until Christ's return
To earth again

5. ## Funeral Complete

Everyday,
People around the world
Depart this fragile stage.
Relatives, friends
And others unknown
Is it in the terror of growing old
That stokes my paranoid reasoning
That death is eying me too?
Long past is my acquaintance with fifty
As I court a life of seventy-three.

However, death's shadow
Keeps lurking about my feet
And with each second of breath

A reminder from the tether
Horns an alarm
That the eminent presence of death
Is forever before me.

The equalizer, a stalker in wait
Ascertained with notice of a repugnant ad
Boarding on the street
"Funeral Complete
All arrangements for a small fee
Three thousand nine hundred
And ninety nine dollars"

A distasteful subject
But, one with absolute finality
Like the warmth of the sun
Rises to morning in the East
Bowing in the evening
To slumber in the West
And this aging body one day
Darkness will detain in a lengthy rest.

Devout love for the Almighty
I sincerely profess
To the family, with respect I attest
Setting my affairs in order
With the request of my bequeath

For this earthly life will assuredly end
Unconscious in perpetual sleep with the dead.
Until the Life Giver
Calls me from the grave
On that glorious resurrection day

6.   Blackbird Games

Blackbirds circling in
Transient from out of town
Honorable males dominate the pact
Accompanied
By the red breast spot female
Adorning her crown

Ruffling, rumbling, are the sounds
Announcing, Blackbirds' gathering
Unwelcome, trespassing
Fall picnicking on private grounds
A vast flock on their feet
Rolling in my back yard to feed
Turning over leaves scratching the ground
Furiously foraging for food to be found.

There's a fright of so many.
It's like daylight blackness
That from inside my house
I steadily tap on the windowpane
High they fly into the trees.
Minutes later they break for ground.
Again I tap on the windowpane.
And again we play the same game.

Until the flock decides to gather,
Continuing that journey South
Seeking a winter retreat
Away from the icy ponds
And wintry snow beneath their feet

Blackbirds, I am glad to see you go;
Small is my backyard.
It will not accommodate the lot of the whole,
Migrating in droves

Under God's traveling grace
Hurry, continue your way
Voice your sounds of "oke-a-lee"
Speak your hellos and good-byes
Southward Blackbirds fly.

7. *An Honorarium*

The eyes, heart and soul
Are eager to greet and please
Acknowledging the accomplishments
Of those "Faithful Servants,
Diligently Laboring in the Vineyard"
Traveling God's Social Circuit
"Sharing His Holy Word"
And opening the Banquet Hall
To forgotten, but valued souls.

8. *The Winter Snow*

There is calmness and peace
When the winter snow
Blankets the land
A reminder of the serenity of love
The sanctity of home
The coziness of chilled air
Presently enjoyed

But, winters' icy white coat
Can drag weariness onto welcome
Storming around too long
Holding Spring to a crawl

While its frosty train
Grabbles on frozen ground
Delaying
The commanded transformation
Of speedily melting into fresh water
Swiftly flowing downstream

Rushing to quench the thirst
Of low valley dry lakes
Anxiously waiting
For a refreshing spring run

To make possible work
For the planting and growing of crops
As the new season takes its turn
And happily bids goodbye

To a Snowy Winter
That has proudly lost
Its seasonal temporary home
But, found a new one
And transitioned to liquidity
Until the next Winter snow is born

9.   Tomorrow

If today is my tomorrow
And without notice
Jesus Decided to Knock
On my door

Whether today or tomorrow
Will I be ashamed?
Inviting Him in

Will I offer Him?
A place at my table to eat

Will I offer Him?
A comfortable Room
To rest and sleep
Will His visit Bring Joy?
And warmth to my Home

Or,

Will I just not open the door?

Pretending to be gone
Worrying about preparations
I should have done

For tomorrow is without promise
Yet, I do have today

With the Blessings
Of His Eternity
Sealed when He rose
From the dark menacing Grave.

10. *An Inheritance Awaits*

Jesus' Resurrection from the dead
New birth into a living hope
A promised inheritance
Salvation to those who believe
Endowed with God's Mercy and Grace

An abundance of treasure
Veiled by silken clouds
Mysteriously secured in heaven
Under a majestic security shield
That man's powers cannot flinch
Disease spoil, fire destroy or time fade

A grandiose inheritance
To be awarded
With a crown to rest
Upon heads of heirs
Enduring against temptations
Persevering under trials

Faithfully staying the course
Pacing the last leg
Of the un-comprising victory race
Celebrating in dance and song
Their delight in God's Love

For we can be sure
He keeps His Promise
Of the Eternal View.

II.   I Long For You

I am forced to live in a world,
Without the presence of you
I wake each morning
Looking out the bedroom window
Admiring the flowers in bloom
My joyful reminder of you

I remember,
Your image towering over me
Those bright hazel eyes
That strikingly, handsome face
The embracing of those long arms
Wrapped in one lasting hug
A gift of four sweet words
"I Love You Mom"

Your picture sits in the curio cabinet
And there it will remain
Your memory is woven in my heart.
Binding fragments
Of a garment ripped apart.

Your death I have accepted.
The hurt has been unbearable.
The pain to my body
A carcass with an opened wound
Cleansed with grief loving tears
Bandaged in forgiveness
The healing of eight long years

Tending my garden of flowers
I feel the quintessence of you.
I inhale and exhale life's fragrant beauty.
My thoughts reaching out for you
A reminder,
That you are no longer here
The choice was yours
Our precious love one
With memories so dear
Our love we send
Express to you, replete with
Mom, Dad and Sister tenderness
While you sleep.

12. **Cherished and Loved**

Having slipped through your hands
Shattered the family portrait
Fell to the floor;
Crash and the drinking glass
Splatters everywhere
Unlike your heart
These earthly things
Need not be repaired.

Aspirations and dreams
Are not always modeled
To our way of thinking
Yet, God in His infinite Love
For you and this family
Has ordered our life,
In a special way
That we can surely trust
And in Him obey.

Your sight often migrates
To a blinding view
Of the family love
And support for you
As you shell up like a turtle
Entombing the beautiful you

The flowers in the garden
That you love so
Do not control how they grow.
However, it is God's will.
Oh how their lovely existence delights you.

"The Lord is compassionate and gracious"
(Psalm 103:8)

He teaches me to tenderly nurture the garden
With bountiful smiles and hugs
Beginning each day with heavenly joy
Coalescing faithfully in precious love.
You travel not this journey alone;
I will always cuddle you in my arms
And God with powers beyond this earth
Will give us the strength
To remain prayerfully strong,
Trusting I gift to you my dear
This treasure of a poem, written
From the heart of your MOM.

13. Poetry and Song
     A Tribute to His Mom

A life celebration
A tribute to his mom in poem
A rendering
To the beautiful person, he called mom,
Known for giving her heart to Family and God,
Spiritually gifted in song
A nightingale whispering tunes
For a mother and culinary artist
Who spoke savory taste buds into bloom.

Holding back the tears
He is reminded of her lively years
As he utters charming words
Expressions of dearness poured from his heart,
Sweetened by honey phrases in rhyme
Repertoires of her works in song
Earthly memories of a life,
A dedication to a virtuous woman.

Weeping, he tenderly smiles,
Dries his eyes and sang goodbye mom.
Then speaking in an undertone groan
He sighs "See you when I make it home."
The pink and white coffin sealed,
While mom in silence so sweet
Takes her seat too around God's Throne.

Chapter 2 - Memorable Treats

I. **Bitter Not Sweet**

Elongated with a polished color of yellow
No glaring blemishes on its face
The strange inviting fruit clings to the tree
Its magnificent semblance is hypnotizing
And I am not blind, nor foolishly deceived.

Desirous of a flavor incredibly unique
The luscious rind of the enchanting lemon
Seduces my mouth -watering eyes to eat
And instantaneously
The acidic lemon juice tingles my teeth

Parting, engulfing the juice
Impeding the seeds,
Inward I suck my jaws
Twist my sour tongue,
Lick the tartness from my lips,
Spluttering that I don't need.
Then solemnly and powerlessly tearing ,
I imbibe a sobering lesson in lust

With mementos to remind
That the spur of bitterness
Is repugnant to the palate of sweetness;
And life becomes a discovery
As it is mysteriously uncovered,
Innocently touched
And purposefully seen
For what it is
Joyful, Bitter and Sweet.

2. Three Yeast Cakes

She yelled to my mother
From across her back yard,
Send Earline to see me,
My queue for a run to the corner store.
I really didn't mind
For she was mysterious and
I thought it fun and adventurous
To walk through the overgrown
Brushy narrow path to her home.

Then waiting before knocking
On the chicken wire screened,
Latched back door
I would quietly listen
With curiosity

To the sound of her voice,
As she conversed with others.
I never knew or wanted to see.

Always bewildered, I would holler.
"Mrs. Jackson!" I'm here!
And a lonely, old and crouched,
Cinnamon faced wrinkled, lonely lady
Would slowly creep and limp to the door,
Tightly gripping her walking cane
In her arthritic twisted hand.

Expecting me, and my southern politeness
She readily let me in,
Handing me her folded
Tattered, scratch paper,
Wrapped around three bills
She would utter,
"Don't forget to bring me my change back"

Easing out the front door
Merrily, I skipped to the store,
Bringing back treasures
She so urgently implored.
Three yeast cakes, a can of malt syrup
Three Irish potatoes, sugar in a five lb. bag

Fermenting ingredients
Hand churned, mixed and cured
In a large clay pottery jug
A fizzing month's supply
Of Homemade Brew

A murky brownish liquid
Known as "Home Brew"
Sealed in used canning jars
Secretly offered to special neighbors,
For fifty cents a pint
The cost for making next month's batch
 Magical is the moment
To relive childhood memories
Of years ago
And the important role, played
In the life of someone aged
Rising to happiness with
Three Yeast Cakes.

3.   Crackle, Crackle

Crackle, Crackle is the sound
Of old oak wood across the fire
At its best burning bright
That the room it lights
Sparkles in great delight

While kerosene lamps, burn out
Leaving glitters for amber light
My Dear grandmother
With all her love and care,
Made sure that together
We said our nightly prayers
Before bedding down for the night

Tightly dressed in a flannel gown
With the fragrance of tallow and turpentine
Soothing across my chest
As the vapors of the mixture danced up and down
Whirling through my nostrils
While my body idled to rest
On a hand stuffed cotton mattress
With a feather pillow for a headdress

And I, neatly tucked under the quilts
In my own comfortable warm space
Feeling the presence
Of my grandmother's gentleness
Smoothing the layered covers around my face
And placing her arm across my waist
Her assurance to me, that I would be safe

With a whisper, "I love you"
She kissed my forehead
And to God, we said
One more Good Night.

4.   *Memories of Christmas Eve*

Gyrating is the flow of Christmas
Joyous is the loving spirit felt
For there is a living God, who cares
With omnipresence that possesses the air
This, my favorite Holiday Season
Cherished and celebrated for joyful reasons
Cradling the heart of traditions so dear
Makes for such a treasured time of the year.

Our house is brightly lit,
Filled with the warmth of Christmas Cheer
Dashing strings of lights flashing red and green
Blink at the bright stars twinkling from the cedar tree
A festive backdrop for the outside holiday scene

Christmas songs on Christmas Eve
The melody of candlelight softly flickers
As garlands and bulbs are hung
Fragrances of gingerbread melt the air.
And scented pine-cones are nestled with flare
Be blessed, it's Christmas Eve
No time for sadness or feeling alone
With family and friends is where we belong.

A sumptuous smorgasbord of Christmas delights
Awaits the arrival of large appetites.
The doorbell dings and Christmas bells ring.
Mom's hot apple cider brews to a steep
Inviting all guest to the table to feast
And enjoy an array of celebrated cultured treats.

Chicken wings, chitterlings, and collard greens
Seafood gumbo, fried fish and lobster tails,
Homemade chocolate cake and pecan pie

Spinach dip, and a casserole or two
Let us not forget those good healthy foods.
Circle the table, just eat, eat and eat.
There is more to name, than watering mouths speak.
Be Thankful it's Christmas Eve

Rejoice and enjoy, herald the joys of peace
God has blessed us most abundantly.
We give to Him all, our honor and praise.
Prayerfully cheering in Christmas Day
It is the birth of Jesus His Precious Son
That we celebrate and happily share
The gift of love with His people everywhere

5.   The Hearth of Caring Love

Toddling in gaiety
Tugging at the sash
Dangling from her faded print-dress,
Babbling grand mama, grand mama

Happily, she reached down smiling
As I wormed around her legs and feet.
Excitedly she lifted me.
Loosened the maiden apron strings
From her skirted waist
And in the coziness of her motherly arms
She cuddled me close to her bosom.

Oh how I felt cherished
Snuggled in the warmth
Of the starchy white apron blanketing me
My first fond memories of caring love

Astonished how the years
Have swiftly advanced
And I retreating
In my mountain top home
Firmly fixed
In front of the gray stone fireplace
Engrossed in precious thoughts
Of my grandma
And how we would in her golden years
Just sit, talk and rock.
And I would always marvel
At the fireplace, she everyday
Lovingly, and meticulously whitewashed

Romantic is this rainy fall night.
The wet oak wood on the soothing fire
Crackles and pops
And I, refreshed with the now
Gaze daringly at the iridescent flames
Enchanted by twinkles of embers

Resting peacefully on the hearth
Cradled in cooled ashes
Awaiting a kind breath to flicker a spark

And you with compassionate arms of love
Sing whispers of lasting precious words
    "I love you"
Tenderly spoken in sincerity
Blending humility and respect
To warm the heart forever
With new fond memories of caring love

6. **Different Worlds**

Sometimes there exists within our lives
Two very distinct and different worlds,
Bounded to the nature of their character
Bearing the semblance of night and day
And yet the ability to love
Shines light upon each face

Differences are notably unique
Sometimes the presence of one
And the absence of the other
Triggers the heart to feel bleak
One is patient, caring and expressive
The other is impatient, selfish and suppressive.

In the center of these parallel worlds
Travels I, the wandering nave
Searching for a way to fulfill my dreams
Of playful days and romantic nights
Dispelling the bleakness of darkness
For the charming emotional brightness
Of the warmish sunlight
That I so desperately desire,
A prelude to the crescendo
Rising in my soul.

7. **Snow In Georgia**

Great is the news
Of our incoming guest
His presence will award us
With the assurance
Of extra hours of holiday rest

Acknowledging the arrival
We rush stores
Shopping for favorite foods to eat
Water, milk and juices to drink
Portable heaters and fuel for heat
Flashlight batteries and candles for light
Music and games for family fun and play
Books to read and photos to take
Equipping for unforeseen togetherness
Prompted by inclement weather

Willingly,
We prepare ourselves for the force
Of this visitor's strong icy arms
Faithfully praying that he will come
Wondering if the weather anchor
Sounded the right alarm
Hoping that Mr. Snowy won't stay too long
Puffing deep freezing ice
Disrupting the mild winter comfort of home

Unlike Easter, Christmas or New Year's Day
We know what to expect
And the extent of the stay
But when snow visits Georgia
Our southern hospitality is exquisite
Given a twenty-four hour day
Then it's time to pleasantly bid goodbye
Sending the white, icy, flaky visitor
Packing north, express without delay.

Chapter 3 - God's Smile

I. *Aspiring Love*

My body is the hearth
God has provided
My soul is the kindling
He supplies

The flame is you, my dear
Glowing fire
Fueling my heart
With desire
Refining and bonding
Our ardent love
With a tranquilizing
Hearth fire
Of comfort and warmth

Lovingly adored
Passionately aspired
By the heavens above
Sweetly we laugh
Joyfully we cry
Together we are blessed
In the richness of life–
All God Inspired.

2. *The Promise*

Darkened eyes embrace a love
That a seeing man might fear
For blinded faith is
The sighted hope
That my God's Love is real

3. *God's Smile*

The virtues of Christian Love
Are absorbed in the Fruit of the Spirit
Daily seen in our faithfulness
To God Our Father
With celebrations of Prayer and Praise

4. *Praying For You*

When you feel that no one cares
Be blessed to know
That there are those afar
With a presence so near
Praying for you
The Blessings of God's
Almighty and Precious Will

5. *May Your Faith in Him Never Sway*

He is the Hope of comfort and peace
Ordering the freshness of Love's relay
Without fainting
Eagerly we run each race

In anticipation of a victory
With the reward being
A spiritual newness
Found only in experiencing
An boundless Love
In Christ Himself
And His enduring Grace.

6.   A Special Thank You

With tears of blessing
Streaming down my cheeks
I smile in cheerful silence
To express a Special Thank you
From the depths
Of my grateful heart

Oh, how your sincere words
Caressed my despairing soul
With the soothing warmth
Of God's immensely showered
Love.

7.   Thankful for Life

Our journey may not be easy
Nor may the byways be safe
Purposeful is our living
With God directing the way
It is in God we trust
It is God, to whom we pray
Offering Thanksgiving with Praise
For His Blessings of Life
Not only for this moment
But for all our full,
Breath filled days.

8. God's Forgiveness

Crystal clear is the cool water
Springing from the mountainside
Flowing with a smooth ripple
Swishing soft bubbling sounds
Purifying barriers to repentance
Waiting to be whitened
In the forgiveness of Divine Love

Thank God
For the purification of new water
Running swiftly under my feet
Pooling, to a mirror reflection

Of an image that represents
Today's blessings
Peacefully seen
Tomorrow's promises
Of joyful hope

Vanished is the gloom
Of yesterdays' mistakes
By the Blood of the Lamb
My errors are all washed away

God has shown forgiving mercy
And through salvation
Granted me His Grace
Obediently, my life will be lived
On the commands I must keep
And the promises He has made
To keep me safe at His Feet.

9.   The Potter's Show Case

LORD,
I feel extremely blessed
You have revealed to me
True wisdom
With an understanding of your ways

Faithfully, I Pray
For the quietness of voice
The sweetness of tongue
The soft laughter
Of an enthusiastic spirit
That excites wonder
And joy in others

Like ants tracking
The sweet scent of candy
It was just a few months ago
When grief scented
With bitter shame

Cast me down
Several ominous roads
My life was a dread
From day to day
Sinking me deep
Into a portable grave

Oh God,
Thanks be to You
For a Sweet Savior
I found in Christ
A light illuminating my path

With an overflowing
Of the Holy Ghost
Propelling my weakened gait

Yes Lord, I am blessed
Your miracle display
Strengthened with a renewed spirit
Of awe-inspiring Mercy and Grace
Empowered,
With reinvigorating Divine Love
Crafted, refined and reshaped
For the Potter's show case.

10. *God Is Forever Faithful*

Sealing the murky humidity
Against Summer's haze of uncharted heat
Dimming the vivaciousness of the morning sun
Silvery misty clouds lowly stand aloof

Routinely, I stroll on callused feet
Nourishing this body with fresh air for breath
Engaging, a mind that has a heart to see
A caring soul that has the knowledge to hear
And the wisdom to feel
The Voice and Spirit of God's Sweet Love
Even under skies dimmed and bleak

From the shadowy midst
Of a gloomy bus stop
I saw her shivering
With gripped hands
Back and forth on tiptoes

Peering upwards
To mummer a quiet prayer
As though she was, closet enclosed
Literally unaware that I was even there

Smiling, I chanced her eyes
To say, "Send one up for me"
She replied "Okay"
Mutually agreeing to pray for one another
We each felt Blessed
Journeying to our destinations
Thanking the Lord with joyful praise

Downcast may be the mood
Of an overshadowing opaque day
That threatens to dampen hope
With a dismal, grim stillness
Offering a dismal uneasiness
To being obedient to the faith

But Blessed is the man
Who can look to the Heavens
Knowing that God our Creator

Is Faithful to all His Promises
"And Loving toward all He has Made"
(Forever sealed by the Sacrifice He Paid).
(Psalm 145: 13 NIV)

II.   **Thinking of you, Welcoming Days**

Yesterday's cloudy skies
May have snatched the sun's
Brightest hue
Yet the sighted warmth of daylight
By the Creator's Command
Is not to be removed

Today the forecast is rain again
For a mild rinsing of the pain endured
Knowing that His rainbow
Will smile through across the sky
Renewing the hope of our faith
In Divine Love to our Living Christ

Knowing that better days, will soon be
Even with down pours of flooding rain
For underneath the mist of unsettling clouds
Our Holy Father has a blast of sunshine
Eagerly awaiting to cheerfully illuminate
The peaceful joy of our welcoming days.

12.   **The Pleasure Of Fishing**

Sitting on the bank
Of a friend's pond
Enjoying the open air
Listening to the frogs cluck and croak
While the birds flying around sing their tunes
Taking notice of the glowing dogwoods in bloom
Focusing on the grayness of the hardwoods that surround
And their appearance of being bare

As if someone forgot to mention
That spring is in the air.

What a quite pleasant afternoon
The wind sending a soft breeze through
Blowing the coolness on my face
As it takes hold of the water
And creates its subtle waves.

And I holding my fishing pole
Relaxing and reposing my mind
Enjoying the peace and tranquility
While simultaneously waiting for a fish or two

Just to bite my bait
And sink the red cork on my line
Hoping that there will be a fish I can snatch
And the catch will be mine.

I don't fish all the time.
I'm just delighted for one catch
Hysterical if I hook two
The enjoyment of
Inhaling God's fresh open air
Waiting for a fish
Praying for a bite
To circle through

Thank God for providing
For the fisherman
And the fish too.

Chapter 4 - Adventurous Play

I.   The Forbidden Fruit

Golden is the luscious fruit
Tastefully appearing sweet
Knowing the ease of being deceived
The passer- by quenches his desires of hunger
Quivers and quietly turns to flee

Fearful of lust and greed
He dares not taste of this delicacy
For he knows that it will excite
An arousal of romantic mystery
Savored to be bitter sweet.

However, his hankering appetite yearns
For the bite of his teeth
To refresh in the inviting fruit
Dangling from the forbidden tree

Eyes may see beauty and behold
How the strong hearted is weakened
From deep within the soul,
A love stricken mind struggles for control
And the breach to the prevailing perimeter
Signals an alarm
Perfecting a decree of the moral code

2.   The Romance of A Maple

Soft and fleecy
Elegant and breezy
Astounding is the poetic canopy
Seemingly smiling vivaciously
As the harvest sun cascades

Upon the compact leaves
Of this stately stunning tree

Arching in the early spring
With fresh sprouts of bright green
Glazing to a thickness under the summer heat
A shade invitation for a lover's retreat

Indescribable is its fall habitat
Tinged with golden sensuous appeal
Spruced with a delight of sophistication
Lovingly adorned with zest
Breathtaking, holding the heart captive
Seducing each sight-seer at will

Until nature surprisingly swirl's its wand
Then floating and drifting moisture dry
Shriveling golden leaves quietly transform.
From gold to a tarnished bronze

Finding rapture with the earth they expire
Leaving the awesome tree
Comatose under the grayness of callus bark
Until winter dispels its dismal sleep
And spring days kneel to the sun's release
Of radiance as temperatures upward creep

Trinkets of green leaves bud on rousing branches
Like fringes flouncing from a lavish parasol
Dangling, soothing the Mermaid ribbed legs
Trunk and root of this succulent maple tree

3.   This Harmony of Love

Mastering bravely through the quietness
Engaging his strong masculine fingers
He gazes gently into her intriguing eyes
Lifts his white satiny table napkin
And genteelly captures a blossoming tear
Symbolic of a caring love
Purposefully blind to the onus of fear

A regal invitation penned
In the aromatic fragrance of love
Two hearts coalesced in the aura
Of romance emulsifying their world
Driven by the intimacy of uniting spirits
Desirous of a quiet cloistered adventure
Where the congenial ecstatic taste for the hour
Reveals their pleasurable fondness
To the loving prudence
Awarded the care of rare flowers

Fascinating is the unique nature
Of these pristine treasured moments
Romantically intensified by the fervor
Of the heart's intangibles
Happiness and joy
Mellowed, preserved and sealed
With the full richness of enchanting ambiance
Mystified in the glints of the candle glow
Blissful is twilight with stared twinkles
Reveling at the pace of the waxy flow

Osculating lips passionately impinge
Modeling petals of a sweetheart rose
Casting light shadows on cupid curves

With luscious breathless wet kisses
Mystically sweeten into sparkles
Seducing entreating hearts
To sip and dine
On warm aesthetic delicacies of passion
Simmered in sparkling mix fruited wine

Captivating is this esteemed rapture
With an unrelenting desire
That refuses to be denied
The insatiable euphoric sensation
Of an unforgettable oasis of pleasure
That pulsates in rhythmic harmony
With the sensual excitement
Of truly passionate Love.

4. *Am I A Priceless love?*

If my love requires a ransom
Then our bond of trust
Lies as flattened, silent drums
And I your most irreplaceable possession
Skillfully survives being your valuable pawn

Tingling the cymbals of selfishness prevail
Without piping, the chimes of compassion fail
A lonely heart struggles to treble
Denied the kindness of friendship
Desirous of a precious jewel
Waiting to be polished and treasured

Can you imagine I
Upon your pedestal
Cuddled in the strength
Of encouraging and protecting arms

Announcing to the world
That ours is a priceless love?

Freely given and exquisitely received
Filled with a passionate hunger to please
Its value is a measure of sincerity and care
And actions that say
For you my dear, I'll always be there
Trust and depend on me.

5. *A Mediterranean Moment*

Wonderful thoughts of happiness
Sends love flowing our way
With fond memories
Of our meeting new friends yesterday
Tenderly, we held our lover's hands
Honoring exact yet humble demands
Going about life each day
With our expressions of love
Proving to be excitingly incredible
And much greater than great

With our faces being stroked by the sunrise,
We review the necessary plans
For the adventures of the day
Then waiting for the ship to anchor
Before we are quickly tendered away.
Off to a strange and exotic island
Just to spend time together this day

Exploring a new and exciting place
As all e-mails have been routed to folders,
With voice mails being held on tape
For we are in a different part of the world,

And home is thousands of miles away.
So we shoulder bottles of water
For the spirit of the body to flourish through
Explorations are tours of the cruise.
Exclusive reservations made in twos
Expiring by the end of the day.
In haste, we rush to the deck
For our ship will embark and leave us astray.

Weary the evening has come to an end
Watchfully, we wait under skies of blue,
Together, standing in the door
On our ocean balcony floor
Looking toward the horizon
At the gorgeous western view
Watching the Mediterranean sunset hide its hue
Waving, we bide good bye, Happy cruising
And God's Blessings be with you

6.   New Friendship

Face to back, Back to face,
One touch, One turn,
And excuse me, we say
With a quick
Face to face.

Our eyes meet
Our lips greet,
We manage
A welcoming hello
With a serious
"How are you today?"
A new friendship made!

Inquiring of a phone number
Accepting the offer
Anxiously awaiting
The call
For a get to know you date.

7.   The Mansion

Viewed for the elegance of cathedral windows
Favored by the goodness of the sunshine
Enamored by the captivating grandeur of life
Expansive is the mansion crested on the hill
Anchored by the edge of the ocean bank
Built on the firmness of a lasting foundation
The silence to the anxiety
Breeding all slippery slope fears

Steel gated is the enclosure that surrounds
This enormous secluded home sacredly bound
A consortium of concealed rooms
Keyed to a life veiled by hampered years
Of uncelebrated accomplishments
And pools of dried heartfelt laborious tears
Pain and grief from those near and dear
To whom love was offered, yet not revered
Being self-centered they had no spare love to give.

Today welded steel gates swing open
Awaiting the honor of your arrival
Blithely welcoming you in
As you my dear are a trusted friend
Worthy of the mansion's precious treasures
Spoken riches, known only to elite friends

Your access requires no knock
For you, unsealed are the rigid tombs
Airy and fragrantly fresh spring aromas
Piped from all corners of the passion scented rooms
Affectionately, I entreat you to follow your instincts
As you randomly choose, the choice does not matter.
All are filled raptures of fortunes
From the heart of the esteemed mansion
Freely unveiling her devotion to you.

8. Sunlight Dancing on Banks Lake

Sitting on the dockside in the cool of the day
Looking across at the clear Black Water Lake
Gloating at the reflection of the regal swamp trees
As they mirror an image on still water so relaxing to see
What a majestically painted view
As the floral prism from the setting sun
Influences the swampy atmospheric hue

In a breath, there is a caress
From a gentle breeze
Inspired by the north wind blowing
Silently through the trees
And as it massages inviting faces
We absorb the harmony and synchronicity
Of mesmerized complete unity
And tranquility graces our every space

Joy of enchantment over-flows in our eyes
While the shimmering reflection of
Brilliant and unrelenting sunlight
Filters through the motionless blue sky,
Smiling down on the Black Water Lake

And the carefully suspended sun
Orchestrates her ardent talent
Stirring the movement of this quiet water
To poignantly refract an illumination
Of moss covered pine and cypress trees
Yes, bright crystal sparklers of light arrayed
And dazzling with the joy of the Spring breeze

In awe and amazement we stare
Entranced by this festive,
Sequestered beauty
Of Nature's eloquent salsa,
Perpetual twirl
Twisting, shaking and turning
With prodigious and perfect symmetry,
Poise and charmingly romantic ease

Blessed we share a moment in time
That embraces the renewed pleasure
Of our deep and ever-binding love,
An unforgettable memento from Above
Yes, this precious gifted treasure
Designed by the artistic Hands
Of Our Kind and Loving God
Special for us to forever behold

Chapter 5 - Claimed Victories

I. *Hope Restored*

"Do not store up
For yourselves treasures on earth"
Where moth and rust destroy (Mt 6:19)
And, the precious valuables
For which one lustful claim
Becomes bundles of mingled trash
Stuffed into tons of plastic bags
The making of a hoarder's nest

A seven room small brick house
Boarding pounds of garbage
With a junk yard outback
While its owner
Takes refuge in the tool shack
Living like a beggar
In need of an income

Unclean and unshaven was he
With worn leather shoes
On frost-bite feet
Rough hands and dirty nails
Requiring potash soap
For cleaning

Thinking of him as insane
Evildoers
Would take his money
Neighbors and friends
Would pass his way and wave
Family
Would hang their head in disgrace

A caring heart moved to town
Sighting

The broken spirit-hearted-hoarder
Graciously she shared her best
Untiringly she worked
Helping
The old man restore his name

With God's Blessings
The shack is abandoned
Junk from the yard removed
The old man's spirits are lifted
He is washed and cleansed
And the house too

Hope is restored
Faith ordered it true
Neighbors of neighbors
Transformed too
When God's truth
Is allowed to resonate
Within the heart
Of boundless friendship.

2.   *The Passenger*

Transporting her taciturn passenger
Cautiously, the old pulp wood truck
Rolled through the opened gate
Slowing in the narrow driveway

Choking on a hesitating clutch
She chugs with a loud pistol backfire
Stopping to seize

Her own familiar
Oil basted parking space

Unlike other times
When the truck bedded him down
The inebriated passenger decides
Not, tonight

With his hand carved pipe
Buoying on droopy lips
He shoves several times
On the driver's door- panel
Intemperately falling
From the old blue dilapidated truck

Lifting himself off the graveled dirt
He lumbers to the back porch
Missing steps and weaving
Indiscriminately tumbling
Inside the sagging door
Where all lights are instantaneously
Pulled to an off–by string cords

Life breathes not a sigh
As twelve frantic feet
Hastily disappear from within sight
Fleeting like frightened mice

The kitchen light jerks on
Then yelps of "get- up"
Are murmured with mumblings of
"Come-fix me something to eat"

And rumblings of
"Come –pull my shoes off my feet"
As if servants were within an ear

Wide awake, listening, waiting
For those grumbling, disturbing sounds
To sleepily disappear–

Not a chance:
As the oldest of the crew
Laggardly warms the food
Serving it on an old stone -chipped plate
With a bottle of Louisiana Bull hot sauce
And a quart size fruit jar of ice water
To squelch the redness from his face

Disgustedly,
The next crew member in line
Grabs and tugs
Removing dusty boots
From corn-bread smelling feet
Dumping them in a corner closet
(Reserved for work clothes)
Of the match-box size farm house

It was only when he was drenched
In his brew
Friday through Saturday
And sometimes Sunday
That this hard working,
Unconventionally schooled man
With an abundance of mother wit
Became a bully of meanness

Inciting frantic calls to God
With desperate pleads
And fervent prayers
To place a rush

On the safe and speedy arrival
Of desired calming peace
That only Monday morning can bring.

Again, the devoted truck
Had dutifully guided her master home
Unaware of the loving rays
Breaking from the setting sun
With disregard for the "we care" stars
Accompanying the grayish moon

However, on this weekend night
Their last venturous drive—
Pre-empted by God—
Ushers in a season for the passenger
Without a halo of glowing light
To crown the awakening of dawn

Dismissed is the early rising
Of Sunday Morning
As for some
Healing begins a new week
As for others
The week-end is muddled in despair

A finality with a visitor
That takes, then quietly goes
A passenger transitioning
Under the grayish glow of the moon

And watchful eyes of countless stars
To a valley beyond
Where only God knows.

3. ## Destination Heaven

She was called naïve
Not because she was easily misled
Nor because of the existence of evil
She often failed to see
Even during times of turmoil
When evil taunts its ill will
 Forbidden is its presence at her table
An air of arrogance, foreign to her senses
Always welcome as an honored guest
Is the Sweet Goodness
Of the Holy Spirit
Anointing her with His wisdom
Instructing her in His ways

With love,
She forgives her enemies
Their cruel worldliness she disdains
Her destination is Heaven
And only God can turn her away

She holds a heavenly ticket
"Faith with Obedience"
Words of a Promise
Stamped, a right to passage

Onward she leaps
Persevering in God's will
Celebrating with praise
The Godly life she has lived
The Holy love she has shared

God's fruit of the Spirit
She has faithfully sown
Being delighted with the harvest

The gates of Heaven open
And there she takes her seat
With the Master
Around His Throne.

4. The Season of Doors

There are seasons
That swing with joyful open doors
There is also a season
When the door swings with a quiet close
A physical death, a transplanting
The crowning of a heavenly awakening
When a loved one departs
For their heavenly home

No matter how hard we try
To prepare our hearts
The difficulties of a loss
Lie deeply in those strands of love
Tender fibers saturated within the soul
That keep us close to the ones we love

Tears of goodbye we will shed
The pain we will try to contain
However, we will grieve
Like the righteous
Faithful in the hope of knowing
The eternal joy of fellowship
Rejoicing with our loved ones
Some day not far ahead.

5. Today

Today I hear life sounds
From attentive ears
That I have never heard before

Today I see from anxious eyes
Once blinded by fear

Today I know of a love
Fresh, transparent and precious
That I never knew could exist

Today I feel the presence of God
In Him a loving companionship
With the promise
That He is forever near

He is the glistening sparkle
The crystal starlight shining
The bright light twinkling
Illuminating my heart

Profusely glowing inward
Igniting an outward spark
With exceedingly great joy

So that this world may know
He is my God,
Always deserving
Of my Honor and Praise
For Today is my Tomorrow
And in Him my Eternity lives

6.   *A Selfishness Unknown To Sacrifice*

When documents are shredded
Proof of evidence is muted
All that's left is paper
Chopped for confetti

Selfishness,
Concern for one's own needs
Voluntary muteness to others
"Who cares, it does not affect me"

Am I not the man - woman?
Created to care for the earth
And commune with God

Am I not my brother's keeper?

Am I not a cheerful giver?

Am I not a believer in Christ?
The Beloved Son of God

Unselfishly He,
Made the Ultimate Sacrifice
Depriving, Himself
Of a royal earthly material filled life

Lifting my arms to the heavens
It is He, whom I extol

His Promises He keeps
The floodgates of heaven open
His Blessings freely pour

Sincerely I commit
To the work of the Lord
Offering myself
A living sacrifice
Pure and complete
"Holy and pleasing to His Word" (Rom12:1 NIV)

7.   The Queen Cleome

The morning sun radiance
Awakes the lovely airy flowers of Cleome
And she in turn responds with gratitude
Gracefully styling
With her blossoms dressed
In salmon-pink layers
Sparkling with a contrast of white
Growing in between her spider leaves
With an iridescence of gaiety
Freshly sweetened by the morning dew
A dramatic scene with a striking view.

As it is the summer's end
The Cleome makes known her tenure
For cooler temperatures
She cannot tolerate
And the hour of her departure
Breathes only of a sigh away,
However, for this moment she will smile
Enjoying the fullness of her blossoms
Then surviving the closing of another day
She will prayerfully fold her petals
In hopes of opening them
To a skyward rising tomorrow

The warming sun beams
Cascading from the calm azure
Delivers flourishing rays
Of natural nourishment to the queen
Fresh and vibrant she is seen
By the pleasing eyes of the handsome bee
Accosting her presumptuously
Showering his cologne about her
An inscription to honor, his precious find

He licks and sucks the Queen's sweet nectar
Immersing himself with yellow puffs
Of thick luscious pollen powder
Passionate souvenirs of love
Tucked in hairs of his black skin coat
His rapacious and selfish desires
Leave little of the Queen's sweetness behind

Enslaved is he by fear
That today may be his last casting time
At Queen Cleome's table to delightfully dine

For autumn is trumpeting a high pitch lyric
And winter will soon drum cold air around
The bee's fate destined- a fatal sleep
While Queen Cleome takes a spellbound rest
Transitioning to a seedpod
Until her spring awakening,
A renewal of her presence and her role
In satisfying nature
With the purest devotion of love

8. ## Holding On

    Battling the forces of despair
    Perforating our emotions into a tear
    Disfigured we are being pulled apart
    Clinging to each other tightly
    We vow not to let go.

    Unyielding we hold on,
    Purposefully to show
    That the love shared by hearts,
    Receiving blessings from God
    Is more masterfully powered
    Than a conflicting sea of tension
    That threatens our lives with discord.

9. ## The Solitude of the Sea

    No matter where I am in life
    Or what my stature may be
    There are times when I feel this loneliness,
    With something tugging at me
    Frantically beckoning me to the sea
    To an unknown world that truly, understands
    The thoughts of my mind
    And what makes me, me.

    The mystery lies within me deep
    As I search for words to express in speech
    Knowing that my inner most feelings
    Linger, buried beneath
    Tons of unfathomable emotions hidden within me.
    I connect to the rumbling of the roaring sea
    As the fingers of the waves reach out for me

Forcing me from the sandy beach
Into the comfort of the deep
Where I relish in peace
As the salty blue liquid flows over me.

Vulnerable and listless
To the desires of the waves
As they mystify and capture me
With pleasure and solace,
Thrilled by the joy of enormous secrecy
Declining to resist willingly, I surrender
To the Solitude of the sea
And reveal the inner me
For choosing to still be.

10. *Old Friend What If-New Friend This Is*

I refuse to think. "What if,"
Leaving the sins
Of "What if" to you
My life today
Is symbolic of "This is"
And "What if" from my sight
Has been banished.

I met "What if" long ago
Traveling with uncertainty
Down dusty rugged roads
Circling, going nowhere
In search of phantom gold
Instead of seeking, The Only One
The object of my heart and soul

I circled and circled
Until one day looking down
I saw, old worn shoes
As coverings for my aching feet
Lifting my head up, I saw
The markings of a street sign
"Comfort and Peace"

I walked without a limp
Down this paved street
Not knowing that a new friend
"This is" I would meet
My heart heard words of Comfort.
My soul felt the spirit of Peace.

The old friend "What if"
Was shouldered a release
Vowing never to look back
God's Angel guided me
Down the glittering streets
Of Comfort and Peace
Joy flowed through my soul,
Injecting full life into my story told
Of God's Gift of Faith lifting me.

II.   *My Faith Walk With God*

It was yesterday,
When misty clouds, presided over dreary skies
And the morning sun being shadowed by a foggy haze
Masterfully summoned daylight's vigor for support
And I, distressed and deeply troubled
Snuggled with the earthworms under dirt

But, this morning when I awakened
The radiant rays from the sun
Provided a warm soothing embrace
That expunged the cold veil of trouble
Lacing me in yesterday's pain

Today a mild Summer breeze
Tenderly caresses and tickles my face
And I looking upward toward the Heavens
Shamefully confess my errant ways
Revealing my need for earnest faith

Suddenly a mirror image flashes before me
And the Holy Spirit enlightens me
Anointing me with Mercy and Grace
Humbly I walk faithfully in His way
Knowing that He has made known
To me
His purpose for life so great

It is in you Oh Lord I lift up my soul
It is in you Oh God I Trust
It is in you Almighty One
That I find Hope and Peace
With everlasting Love
To keep me ever close to Thee
In sweet sleep 'til morn adorns the sky.

Chapter 6 - Affirmations

I. **The Unruly Cloud Attacks The Moon**

Looking upwards toward the heavens
As I traveled home in the pit of night
I saw a runaway adolescent cloud
Devilishly playing,
Trying to deface the Harvest Moon

I watched as the jealous dusty cloud
Heckled, horse playing around
Sliding his gray powdery mass
Across the planet moon's face
Slicing this adult's head with the brain encased

Moments later the cranium reoccupies
His rightful place
The naughty gray cloud playing rough
Circles, attacks the humble moon
Tightens his grip to disfigure
The completeness
Of the moon's planetary shape

Being blindfolded and tied
The moon again escapes
But the streaky mousy cloud
Continues puffing gray smoke
In the stately moon's path
Dividing the moon by unusual means
Under the belt line below the waist
A division of two crescents in one place

Finally, after much rumbling
Celestial bodies vocalize their objections
The stars began to blink
Twinkling their bright lights
The oxford gray clouds of elders

Summoned a call to order
Chastising the young renegade
For daunting and disrespecting
The authority of the moon

Seeing harmony across the clear skies
Filled with a gift of tranquility
In calmness concluding my drive
The moon was again peacefully whole
Rejoicing in his grandeur
Like a milky pearl lamplight globe
Shining with perfect fullness
In the sanctity of his ordained home.

2. The Sting of the Insidious Leaf

I felt a tingle as my face slid by
I felt my lips tighten,
And I wondered why
I could feel them knot up in size,
As you and I
Hurriedly, spurned goodbye.

If I had only worn my floppy hat,
To shield my face
Then my lips would have not been a victim,
Exposed to the prickle of your embrace.

I dared not to use my arms and hands,
For they were hidden,
Sheltered by coverings
Of long shirt shelves
And garden gloves matted and stiff
The itching from your touch

They wanted to escape
Knowing that the clothing
Would be easy bait.

With the sweat pouring from my forehead
gushing onto my face
I vacillated with fear, to wipe it away,
I dared not touch the drop on my lips
For I knew that you, this insidious leaf,
Spontaneously had placed a gentle kiss on me
Just as the morning dew kissed you.
But, without the sting of sap,
That my lips bore from you.

The sweat dried
Leaving crystals of salt
To soothe the ting on my face
My lips returned to normal,

Healing from the brush
Of a delicate touch from you
The poison oak
That momentarily seized me.

3.   Terrorized By A Gnat

A tiny hairy fuzzy gnat
Lives on the corner
Patrolling thirty feet of the street
And when I walk pass
His residence,
He recognizes me.

Annoyingly,
He quickly buzzes
And spins in my face
Spreading his terror
Sensing my fear
Whirling over my head
Humming from ear to ear.

Without luck,
I try using my quarter inch
Dowel walking stick,
To slap him on the head
Trying to avoid
The deadly sting of his bite,
A terrorizing thought to me.

Advancing to a speedy jog
While swinging and fanning
Trying to clobber the ferocious gnat,
Fighting my way beyond
The thirty feet of his path

Regaining normal composure
I slowed, walking, a moderate pace,
Fearing not the gnat
For I was no longer a trespasser,
On a gnat's private estate

4. *A Painting Of Fall*

Enchanting is the fragrance of this moment
The aroma of morning pleasantries all around
Delighting humbly in the caresses
Of soft whispers from the satin breeze
Teasing my hair while kissing my rosy cheeks

Yes, I have patiently waited
For this sauntering splendor of Summer
To ceremoniously retreat.
Humbly I embrace Fall's quiet awakening
With a door knock and gracefully curtsying
To announce her commune with all.
A formality of protocol
You would think or suppose
But every creature large and small
Knows such is to the contrary:
For it is a quiet recline for one,
And a resounding awakening for still another;
The acknowledgment to the existence of all

Endearing is nature's prevailing Fall beauty
A contralto of harmonious richness,
Gifted in earth tone colors
Primed in coats of Autumn's repeating love
Brilliantly soaked bushes, trees and leaves
Lavished in vibrant strokes of orange, red
Gold, rust and brown
All accenting variegated shades of Fall green,
Staring in frantic amazement at the chilled ground
Clinging remorsefully to that liveliness of life
Then gazing upward under the haze
Of dancing sunbeams is

Mingled pine needles and pine-cones
Nestled in bedding straw, left to serve
Its purpose as we are all called.

Spectacular is the immense charm and acts of reminders
Cast against the celebrated backdrop of
Delicate imbued blushes
They too waltzing to the stir
Of the ripening of the golden harvest

For which my heart yearns and seeks
And calls to a life of tranquility
This joyous birthing, "A Painting of Fall"

5. *An Autumn Leaf*

There is a journey that I must take
Which offers me an escape
Where I can pretend
That I am an autumn leaf

Floating gently through the air
Without a worry or care
Just gliding on the breeze
Of autumn's gentle smile
As I journey from here to there.

Traveling many miles a day
Greeting friends and chuckling
As the tip of my autumn leaf
Brushes and tickles faces
While eyes of wonderment
Express excitement in seeing
A vivid orange autumn leaf

With zest and grace, floating
In search of a winter home
A place to recline and rest,
Such an autumn leaf at last
Bonding with earth
Making fertile soil stronger,
Leaving memories blanketed
In special treasured chests

6. Blessed Are Our Days

Blessed are the days of our lives
Although sometimes
Around a corner trouble hides
Just waiting to show its face
To overshadow our joy
With dark colors of plaster and paste

But as always
We look to the Heavens above
For we know
That there is a God of Love
Who sends the rain,
To wash the plaster and paste
Of pain away
Then beckons the sun
From behind troubled clouds
To paste a rainbow across the sky
In remembrance of His Love
For you and me.

7. It Has Been Taken and Given

That which has been given
Is greater than
That which has been taken away
And the emptiness felt
By that which has been taken away
Has been refined into multiple blessings
Filled with peace and remarkable humility

For I know that God is alive
He dwells within my heart

His Breath flows from my nostrils
His unchanging Word is the life
Of my most sacred and secret soul
And I bear witness
That my God, the God of Abraham
The God of Job
Is the One and Only
God I worship and revere.

8.   *Identity In Christ*

Circuitous would be putting it mildly,
For where does one find self
In this maze of life's journey?
We all are seeking to see
Who we want to be as much as
Who we are– and that truly camouflaged.

Always, I acknowledged the name
That my grandmother handed down to me
Followed by branches
From a single family tree
Of a slightly distorted printed genealogy
Revealed, in my search to find
"The why of me"
The unveiling of my true identity

Daring and bold this journey I took
Roaming.
Gaining key portions of ingredients
Supplements for my inherited DNA
A pinch of love, an ounce of trust
A smidgen of faith
Daily prayers to my God

Asking Him to guide my feet
Suddenly, no longer was I
A trampling traveler
In search of the identity of me
For the Holy Spirit's beveled glass mirror
Reflected a radiant image of me
One of semblance, with enormous peace

I found Jesus, yes His Word
By faith, I proclaim
With my mouth, I confess
With my heart, I believe
That He is "Jesus Christ The Lord"
My identity in Christian Genealogy
With roots from,
God The Father, "The Vine-dresser"
Christ, "The True Vine"
His many Followers, "Branches flowing"
Nourished by the Vine
With a branch identifying me.

9. Always and Forever

The trumpet sounds
For all to hear
Our earthly joy invitation
To join Always and Forever,
Both standing motionless
In their gala of a winter's parade,
Rejoicing attempts to join in,
He too has a familiar tone.

Yes, Always and Forever–
Distant cousins

Both share in this family tree;
But only one bears the spectacle
Of time endlessly;
And so we implore
These companions to choose
What will they be–
They must choose, you know.

And because neither would yield
To this humble request so as
To render peace to these feeble souls
Earth had to let out
Her thundering disapproval
And proclaim that:
On earth, Forever often falters
When expressed in love epitomes,
And Always seems to follow,
With razor sharp pain in the very weak.

And so in this isolation
Of mischief and pandering
Of kindred spirits bound by relation,
More than observable with the naked eye
The summons is embraced
Knowing that love
Ordered by the Master Himself
Serves willingly to light our path
And create within us
A dwelling of Eternity
Where Always and Forever
Are enduring pillars for our Sanctity
And God The Father Wills our Victory.

10. Salvation Extended To Me

Facing the rising sun
My soul stands
Determined and strong
Though I cling to cliffs
Of an uncertain life.
Yes, I seek refuge
From the troubles besieging me
Like pendulums on a string

And I dare not slip
In the face of hardships awaiting
To anchor my feet
With weights of sorrow and defeat

Then just as I look upward
To the dome in the sky
Heaven appears before my eyes
And the Hand of God
Reaches out to me
Today my soul is set free

Thank You Merciful Lord
For the victory over defeat
And the salvation that You
Fully extended to me

11. The Timekeeper

Amazingly, cell phones communicate time
Roaming accurately through different zones
An alarm clock often needs rewinding
A grandfather enjoys a twist to chime
A digital, running on electricity

Faithfully displays electronically
And if a wristwatch needs a new battery
There's a risk of lost time

For the human living
The time clock does not stop
For the dead in Christ
There is only a pause in the watch

Unlike man's daylight saving time
Pushed to fall backwards
Jumping to spring forward
As though time lost and gained
Were only thoughts,
That the mind of man changed

And man with all his intellect
Cannot the timepiece of God command
For Only God
Can seize time in the Palms of His Hands.
Remove an earthly soul
From the ground on which it stands
And by His Authority
Death is demanded,
To reassign its plans

Setting the timetable for all events
The Creator calls time into existence
Birthing forth- new life into the world
The timing of His greatness is seen
In the stars shying away
During the light of the day
Giving will to the trusting moon at night
And the magnificent sun for morning light

What an Awesome God we serve
The Controller of Time
The Giver of Life
The stem to the bowels
Of the watch gyrating my soul
Blessing each wisp of breath
That I so gratefully hold.

12. Relationship Prayer

Please God, direct our relationships
With one another
That with each other
We affirm our friendship and love

Embodying the qualities
Of Your Wonderful Spirit
Trusting, Caring, Sharing
The essence of whom we are Forever mindful
That our life's walk
Is oftentimes across a swaying bridge
That we grip tightly in Prayer.

Balancing with elongated arms
Of Hope and Faith, In You, God
That we will not swing loose
Into the mired thicket
Of a world filled with pain and grief.

13.   Encouraged

The Lord awakened me this morning
Speaking in a very special whisper
He filled my heart with joy
Etching in omnipotent kind words
For me to deliver
As encouragement to you

And so, may God's awesome love
Keep you as you make
Painful decisions today
Impacting the lives of others
In such clear and dramatic ways
And even though you may be burdened
By the task you undertake
Just continue to pray and trust God
Each faithful step of the way
For His protection and care
Is Heavenly embraced,
With His abounding Mercy and Grace

14.   God Will Time Us Through

In the bleakest of days
And the darkest of nights
When it appears that there is no one
To care about our plight
As it is the season
Of winter in our lives

Sadly looking from the inside out
Seeing the steam from roof tops choke

Appearing as though
Air vents are puffing smoke
Amidst the cold winter air
Where only a fraction of life itself
Gives way to the appearance
Of looking dull by being bare

We brace ourselves
For the mind troubling thoughts
Of despair
As the catastrophic arrows of life
Penetrate and consume our state

Then from a distant view
The beauty of life pierces through
As the gaiety of the red Camellia
With a vibrant richness
From sun drenched brew
Opens her sweet petals
And exclaims her right to be

Holy Spirit splendor
Refreshment offered to souls
In despair
Re-affirming we knew
That the Love of God blankets us
And times us through

With sun radiant warmth
Comfort and Peace
To each and every family

15.   Hello And Good Bye

Hello, spoken with yesterday's
Pleasant smiles
And joyous expressions
Acknowledging that the advent of this day
Would be filled
With grief and stirring sadness too.

Love and peace creeps in
To help with preparations
For you to reward your loved one
With a Home Going Celebration,
An invitation to family and friends
To respectfully say Good Bye and God Bless
To the life that has peacefully transcended
This temporal estate

Resting, until one day
The Father calls all by name
One by one we rise
And rejoice with sweet hello
And divinely retreat
To everlasting sweet peace.

16.   Another Day

Tweet, Tweet, Tweeter de
Sweet sounds, of the morning
Outside my window
Echoes of colorful song birds
Flickering in the trees

Wake up, wake up, they tweet.
Abandon your sleep;
You have been chosen
Laborers for the Master
This glorious day

Come! Let's fellowship
Come! Let's celebrate
Jesus has awarded you, His servant
Joyful wages of another great day
Holy Seeds have been sown
The harvest is ripe, ready to reap
With opened eyes rejoicing to see
New believers gathered in the fields
A word from Christ they seek to hear
As mission workers worship near

Tweet, tweet, tweeter de
God's songbirds happily sing
Go forth and teach
Calling kingdom builders to the field
A salvation message to preach
Sowers and reapers on their feet
The harvest, soon to ripen
The Holy Spirit moves without a stipend
The Lord proclaims the victory
It's Another Great Day
For all Christian to see
The rewards of being faithful
To Christ, the Just and Kind
Savior and King we all entreat

17. I Silently Prayed

Sitting motionless, I listened to you
Words you were compelled
To utter illuminated
Your troubled life
Yes, you were struggling today

Without you knowing
I understood your deep pain
I felt much sympathy for you
And as you talked, I silently prayed

I see different shades of you
As my heart is touched
By one searching for a place in life
Seeking to find that peace
And harmony for the soul
While screaming out for Christ
Understanding that each day
Adds a little more wisdom our way

And though I am not you
I see myself as I see you
I pray for myself as I pray for you
For I understand the struggles
That you are going through
Oh how I see the challenges before you!

But just remember
In Christ there is saving Grace
He honors us with his Mercy
He has already Won our case
We simply must speak the faith
And in Him find
Comforting peace today.

18. Life And Light In The Wilderness

A pinnacle springtime view
Seen from the uppermost part
Of the mountain peak
A residing thick mass
Of rolling hills, cliffs and valleys
Charming mixtures of embossed green
Towering underneath the Master's seat
Separated by cotton clouds
Layered on a canvas of blue
A small depiction of what God can do.

Even in its massive beauty
The wilderness greenery
Appears difficult to enter through
However, a closer encounter
Reveals many pathways as open venues
Strangely, I discover
How to navigate through.

Bewildered and girdled by the maze
These crossroads of life corner me
With lures and camouflages,
Of great wealth in material things
Down dark wide roads
Of painful hopeless dreams

Suddenly there is this light of life
From the outside barley seen
This is the road of my choosing
The path of my dreams
This road that galvanizes me

Offering shelter
From the roughed wilderness
An invitation to forgiving tears
Welcoming the joy of sunlight
Paging the peaceful rainbow
To beautify the glorious sky
And I am endowed with the treasures
Of love, Joy and Peace
Blessings from God
His Will entrusted to me
For an everlasting harmony
In His Eternity

19. *Forgiven*

He said it; no she said it
Oh, how the tone of a conversation
Dramatically alters
The melody of the heart's pace
Then forces the mind to quake
So that yesterday's troubles
An engineering of small mistakes
Today viewed
As unintentional errors hazing the way.

Noble is the delight of a zephyr
Powered by words of compassion
The prudence of a sincere friend
Boldly mollifying misconceptions
To minute particles of sand
Coarsely flowing through the hand
As forgiven mistakes
Diminished in luster
To minute granules of sea salt

Such a seasoning with palatable taste
To satisfy the heart of a fallen man
As he is lifted to stand

20. To Eulogize

The eyes of the Lord we cannot escape
He rejoices in the good we do
And frowns when we wallow in our mistakes
Forgiveness for our wrongs we must seek
Before we move from this earthly abode
To enjoy eternity with Him
Forever in our heavenly retreat

Often we speak of eulogy
As if speaking of praises
And good will of the dead
Without distorting the truth
For the dead can't hear
Even if words spoken as truth
And sometimes exaggerated in use
And spun in hyperbole

But family members so dear
Mourning the loss of their precious one
So dear
Seeking some comfort from grief
Ask remarks from
The living of the now deceased
A memorable life no doubt
With speech cast years before this night

An inclusion of love and warmth
To the celebration of life

That the deceased once strolled this path
Enjoyed some fond pleasantries
With relatives and friends
Rare tidbits- expressions of life
On earth's canvas painted release.

For each act of wrong that's done
There was always time
For unfolding some great good
Only if we would choose
Such gift hastily and not resist

Hidden deeply within each soul
There in silent secrecy
Resides faith and hope
A trust that filters through
To our greatest joys
And righteousness
In what we have said and done
To lead someone to The Holy One
While life still breathes
And this commission of a eulogy
Passes underneath the human canopy.

Chapter 7 - Inspirations

I. *Stay In The Race*

Working out on a thread mill
A vigorous walk on a beltway
I really don't like to take
For me, one however I have to make
With the first obstacles to overcome
"Getting Started", two words tied
To the mind in bundles

Of so many excuses
I don't want to, I'm too tired too,
I need to, but I can't do
Once my "not to" reasons are unbundled
Then deciding "I will try"
My body conditioning begins
And I'm on course with a right mindset
I've made preparations to complete the task

When life deals us a difficult blow
Succumb not to the pillar of salt
Let yesterdays rejoicing
Be our motivating force
For healing today's sorrows
As this life's journey is not ours to disrupt

Christ is the Keeper of the course
He is the Eyesight,
You once lost along the way
He Provides
The memory of the fun and laughter
From yesterday
He is the Master
Without Him, we could not sense
The presence of living life abundantly

Sometimes I may question
That I don't know the night
On this side constantly forwardly flows
I have traveled many miles
With just a few more miles to finish my race
I am trusting in the Lord, keeping the faith.
I want to claim my crown of righteousness

That the Lord has in store for me.
On that Great Glorious Day
When It Is Him, I'll Happily embrace.

2.   Walking to Shape

Seven o'clock in the evening
It's a little too late
For a four- mile walk
To lose this Dr Pepper weight
I don't want to go
But, I can't be lax
Walking shoes on
Out the door, on feet and toes

One, two, three, four
Walking stick in hand
Legs on the paved road
Three miles to go

One, two, three
Up the hill I go
Tapping my stick to the road
Two miles to go

One, two
Stretching out the thighs
The hill is steep.
I stagger across the street
One mile to go

One, two, three, four
I make it over the top
Down I go, up I go
Right leg, Left leg
Spot a penny in the road
Drop it in my pocket
One half mile to go

One, two, three, four,
Five, six, seven and eight
Stepping with a brisk pace
I must reach home
By nine twenty-eight
Zero miles to go
Thanks, To You God
For this temple honored
In safe-kept shape.

3.   The Red Wagon

See that rusty, dented red wagon
With the old broken axle,
Lingering in the field over there
In the midst of briers and cockle-burs
With its reddish- black tongue
Thirsted in the earth

I know of its mountainous travels
I understand its lonely and weary stare
Aged and feeling abandoned
It has suffered many grievous tears
Fulfilling its purpose
A carrier of burdens weightier
Than man's back could ever bear

Traveling a paralleled path
I stand in witness for the wagon
Bruising has been a desperate shove up the road
Tugging at a forward roll
Trusting in the hope and faith
That whatever my circumstance
The Love of God was in full control

Momentous strides I have endured
Dashing fast in the wake of the chase
Tip-toeing to a slow maneuver
For a change of pace
Striving for righteousness
Always to stay this course,
Tossing colorful confetti happiness
Joy for the sake of sanity as I go

Unlike this old friend eroding in the field
Enchantingly I age as golden fruit
Nourished by contentment in Christ
For I have learned that His Will
Is much greater than my thoughts of might.
And His Hand guides my life
Forever removed from kinship
To my shabby wagon of burdens
And as my journey nears end
God faithfully carts me to Heaven's Gate
And I lift my arms in Praise
Giving thanks for His overflowing Mercy and Grace.

4. *A Menopausal Experience*

Quickly, it came upon me
I don't know the exact hour
Nor can I remember a particular day
It struck me like a wrecking ball crane
Pounding me excruciatingly hard
Jarring and splattering my insides
Into pinching small particles of sawdust
Willfully being milled and grounded

I never received notice – of the thought
That my dwelling was being demolished
And I was being evicted
For grossly neglecting my place
Until the wrecking crew arrived

Perhaps I was too busy ripping and running
Trying to survive and make money
To see the bags drooping under my eyes
The lines of aging lengthening,
Or stop to check blood pressure
Feel the frequent heart palpitations
Notice the frown from others

Painful were the backaches and neck aches
Patched with several aspirins a day

Unsettling was the confusion in my brain
Often times causing me to lose my way
Puzzling over decisions made

Embarrassing were moments
In public view
Fiercely fanning intense heat
That only I could feel and see

Warming my bottom, circling my waist
Engulfing my torso with violent flames

Humiliating early morning hours 2:00 AM
When only the brawlers were awake
The night sweats brutally attacked
Stripping me of my nighties
Leaving iced cold water flooding my chest

My husband daring not to touch me
For fear I would scream a loud "No"
Just watched, as my desires went to waste
For my hormone range was out of place
Like unwanted toasted bread
Crumbling into dry flakes

The final hour had arrived
My pH level was off balance
Acid burned through my body
Nerves stretched and enlarged
Across my skin
Like plant roots burgeoning
Beyond their given space

Forced, was I to see the reality
Of what was happening to me
Prayerfully I sought help
To retain my dwelling place
With a promise to listen
And always take heed
As my body continues to speak
Unrelentingly to me.

5. **Entrapment of A Dream**

Trapped in a world far from me
In the blindness of a blizzard night
That only you see
I heard the terror of your fear
Yelling screams into my ear
And with each call of my name
Your voice is wretched with pain

With a sudden out-pour comes
"Lord have mercy on me"
I felt a presence within your dream
You were moaning over me

Softly I touched your arm
Without disturbing your sleep
Soothing you in such a way
To let you know that I was safe
Ever present in your sight

I called your name
Waking you from bondage
Captive in the world of nightmares
An entrapment
In a dreadful timeless place
An experience
Of a phantom moment in hell
With no release

Then to be caressed
Into the world reality
Of a good night's sleep
Until the morning awakening
And God Stands you on your feet

Finding that all is well
In the lost memory of a dream
Told through the eyes of me.

6.   *Journey Into Reality*

Standing in the open air
Without a worry or a care
Suddenly, a lighting flash
Twitches the threads known as hair
Lifting them one by one
Revealing a sensitivity
Lured by an electric field's scare

An admission of love
When it is sincerely expressed
And magnified to such strength
As the Muse's unmixed potion
Sending sensations through the body
Tenderly warming the heart

Certain of her own Muse's awakening
With trumpeting vibrations of joy
She innocently delivers a memorable
Pulsation, fusing mind and body
Through neurons reserved for special speech
And they each recline under the watchful eye

Of a synchronized resolve for complete
Devotion to their harmonized unity
And to all others, utter anonymity.

7.   *Musical Fountain*

I am so captivated by you
That the sound of your voice
The caress of your palms
The loving countenance
You wear upon your face
Pulsates my heart
Into a timeless sprint

And I flow like a crystal clear stream
Jetting through
A grandiose musical fountain
Filling its basin
With insatiable fantasies

Then surrendering to
The natural gravitational force
I anxiously await,
Allowing nature to resume control

Knowing all is not consumed today,
I am fully replenished
By the very pleasurable image of you
And each mellifluous charming note
That this musical fountain accrues
With such love and beauty
That my cheerful heart yields
Tranquility
To precious thoughts
And memorable life-times with you.

8. *Am I Sexy?*

Stepping with a runway stroll
Dressed from head to toe
Flinging my black shoulder length,
Implanted Asian hair
Parted bangs swinging across my face
Highlighted with a red rose to charm,
The very next guy named john.

A black laced silk tee- shirt
Pulled over my tucked breasts
D cup for the right effect
Draping my petite waist
With a shiny silver belt

Accenting my black, hip hugger
Short and tight, lip defined pants
Taupe panty-hose
And ankle length black high heel boots

Long dark eyelashes
With blackberry red fingernails
Play diamonds on my fingers
Plastic bracelets dangling
On my arms
A purse with my man's money
Locked on my shoulder
Clutched in my palms

Have I not just described sexy?
Or a young girl doing a street walk
A provocative walking billboard
Parading from one corner
To the next
An open invitation to sell her wares

Trashing her body
Masking the true beauty
Of her tender face
Is the work for the john;
A misguided Imitation of God
And the distorted admiration for you.

9.   Being Deceived

Why mouth false truths?
Why sever the chains of hope?
It's your presence that's needed
You are the fiber optic of support

When you fail to be honest in your replies
You cut the friendship lines
With your childish face and deceitful eyes
Your dishonesty is revealed
Abandoned is the friendship
Concealed is the hurt of a friend
Buried in the heart of the forest
Protected by a grassy field

A simple, honest and truthful reply
Would have saved a friendship
From the humiliation
Of unsavory words spoken
Shielded the covenant of sacredness
That bond of blood and trust
That cherished bridge between family and friends
Which keeps us close to each other
Bringing folded hands together in prayer
With each right and left swing
Of life's swaying bridge.

10. Respectfully "No"

Rather than cut me down
Mulching my emotions into the ground

Just say "no" to my request
Maintaining respect without regrets

Imploring the pureness of our friendship
To intertwine with hearts that trust

Vowing that our love remains sound
Cemented with the joy first found

11. Showing Kindness to Others

Always be kind to others
For you never know the hurt
Of their tragic stories to be told
And the mysteries
Hidden deep within their hearts
Held captive behind sealed doors

Blinded the only realness we may see
Is through stained windows of a personality,
Camouflaged behind tinted pupils
Posturing to acquaintances, all is well
Unknown to friends, truthful details
Of a life rocked by haunting disappointments

Struggling desperately to live in a world,
Often-times numbed to evil's filty stain
With sobbing screams of agony and despair
Stretching forth in prayer
Calling the Lord to anesthetize the pain

Realizing in this world
Only the strong in Christ survive
In Him is that Breath of Love
And ascension to victory.
He discerns our hearts
He understands our plight
It is He Who keeps us
When we journey in the darkness of night
He is the florescent glow
The everlasting Word of Light and Hope.

12.   In Your Face

Angry, heavy young lady
Huffing and puffing
Her nose totted
All in the young slender man's face

His stance is unmovable
His face is swollen
Like that of a stormy cloud
He staggers not
From his grounded space

Using both hands
Instead of pushing
Girlfriend out of his face
He knots his tee-shirt
Around his blue jean-ed waist

Girlfriend loudly yapping
Snaps her head
Twist's her hips,
And wags away

The young man's
Emotional swelling
Simmers to an ease
And without a word being said
He calmly turns, struts ahead
Giving Thanks to God
For an unwavering
And cool tempered release
Of instead.

13. *Blessed and Making It*

An old man aided by four legs
Clinking from one room to another
He folds up two legs,
Walks on three legs
Taps one in front of the other

Strangely appearing
Hopping on two legs
Scratches his head
And wonders,
Where did I lose the other

Wheel chair rolls in
The old man sits with ease
His mind a little bewildered
Thanks to his Uncle "Arthur"
The legs complain of a brush with pain

The old man sings his praises
Stands, Giving Thanks to God

Remembering this morning rising
Feeling the use of his hands and arms
To splash fresh clean water
Over his jubilantly aging face

Stiff and sore are his ailing legs
Showing signs of slowing
To youthfully operate
However, God has made provisions
Help is just a prayer, with an answer waiting

The old man eager not to hesitate
Tadpoles from place to place

Forgetting the thorns and thistles
Of pain to hinder his way
And happily uncle Arthur becomes compliant
And releases its vice-griping hold.

14. *After Dark*

Daylight is closing
Dark is quickly approaching
The sign reads "Exhaust after Dark"

Not Morning, noon or evening
These start and end the day
Then pass on.

In wait of dusk dark
Time out for play
I got it! It makes sense!
After dark speaks to night
Black cloudy, back wood darkness

Without the services
Of city street lights

When white teeth and red eyes
Protruding from a black rain coat
Would scare and spook a ghost

Exhausting distilled spirited water
Serving it to the dead in the cemetery
A path taken, as the short cut home

After pitch dark around midnight
Other than the stars and the moon
Frightened and alone
You're on your own

Of course these are exhausted stories told
By family long ago
Sitting around the pot belly stove
Shelling dry roasted peanuts
Poking fun about after dark rendezvous
That offered them bragging rights
To tales, that other than themselves
And the dearly beloved dead
No one living knows the truth
Of that which was done or said.

15. *Precious Jewels Of Life*

There are Precious Jewels.
In the garden of life
Gems with illustrious
And lasting smiles of love
Giving and sharing of themselves

Embodying the joys
Of happiness to others they bear
The fulfillment of living abundantly
Treasures honored by family and friends
Heartfelt memories without end

Sometimes Precious Jewels appear veiled
Concealed by seeds of ill will
Finding pleasure in trampling and pushing
In a jig-jagged -disturbing sway
One could consider insensitive and crude
All fashioned to blind the heart
With a hazy mist, that smog's the eye
And deceives the mind too

Fret not over such trivia and mischief
For the love of the Master Gardener
Tills ever-so-gently through
Unearthing dry compressed soil
With His strong arms of forgiveness
And the Mercy and Grace of Salvation

Giving leave to the blurred vision
Freeing the heart that the mind gives witness
That our Precious Jewel
Removed from this Life
Has been happily and peacefully transformed
Radiating in the splendor of a Crowned Jewel
Resting in God's Heavenly Garden Above.

16. Inspired

Yearning a desirous gift
A Marian Anderson contralto voice
The thirsty canary vocalizes
In melodic tones of hope
Fluid in beauty is the written word
Exulting phrases from depths
Of a heart waiting to be heard

A fresco of unimaginable colors
Layered and painted
Viewed by the kaleidoscope of the soul
Vividly beaming the brightness
Of glittering gold
Sparkling twinkles of rhyming melodies
Bells of brass chiming harmony
With shivers of fine diamond
And yes, cut crystal glass
My mystical images of poetry
Inspired to the last

With magic the poetic stanzas sing
Readings of a Poet with writing dreamed
God's special favor to me
Treasures to family, friends and acquaintances
With you, I share and give
My legacy of love to shape and console.